ABOUT THE BOOK

Crafted out of the love for the David's Psalms and Proverbs written by Solomon, I've written affirmations to deepen the spiritual bond with God the Father, the Son, and the Holy Spirit.

Turn the pages, read the words, and search the scriptures for additional affirmations that you can share with others.

You're encourage to wake up each morning and begin your day with The Word, The Truth, The Light, and The Way!

I TURN FROM OLD WAYS

In the footsteps of Christ, I turn from old ways accepting the Kingdom of Heaven is near.

Inspired by
Matthew 4:17

2

I ENTER NOW

I enter now through the narrow gate, which few pursue and yet brings life to those who find it.

Inspired by
Matthew 7:14

3

I HAVE BEEN CALLED

I have been called too
repentance, knowing each
sinner must seeks salvation
and the Kingdom of God.

Inspired by
Matthew 9:13

I EMBRACE ALL THINGS

I embrace all things that have been delivered to me by The Father and accept His gift, that is His Son, Jesus Christ.

Inspired by
Matthew 11:27

5

I LISTEN WITH OPEN HEART

It is given to me that I may know the mysteries of the Kingdom of Heaven, I listen with an open heart.

Inspired by
Matthew 13:11

I LOVE THE LORD MY GOD

I love the Lord my God with all my heart, soul, and mind and find purpose in His love.

Inspired by
Matthew 22:37

I EMPOWER MY LIFE

I empower my life with the authority given to me from Heaven, acknowledging the power of Christ within me.

Inspired by
Matthew 28:18

8

I CHOOSE HEALING

I choose healing granted in God's grace that I may minister unto others who need healing.

Inspired by
Mark 1:31

I INVITE HEALING

I invite healing and restoration through the Word of God, there is no time or place which I cannot be transformed and made whole.

Inspired by
Mark 3:5

10

I RELEASE NEGATIVITY

I release negativity, guided by The Holy Spirit, I go about my day, shaking the dust from my feet and trusting the journey of divine goodness.

Inspired by
Mark 6:11

I SHALL NOT PROFIT

I shall not profit if I gain the world, for I will lose my soul and have nothing before God.

Inspired by
Mark 8:36

12

I WILL NOT ALLOW

I will not allow my heart to become a den of thieves, rather a house of prayer.

Inspired by
Mark 11:17

I TAKE HEED

I take heed, watching and praying to know when the time of The Lord has come.

Inspired by
Mark 13:33

14

I WILL LIVE MY PURPOSE

I will live my purpose to share the good news which has been shared with me, that there is love and hope for all.

Inspired by
Mark 16:15

15

I CARRY PEACE

I carry peace in my heart, echoing the angels' song of peace and goodwill toward all mankind.

Inspired by
Luke 2:14

I WELCOME FORGIVENESS

I welcome forgiveness offered through Jesus Christ, trusting in divine grace and love that I can arise and go into His house.

Inspired by
Luke 5:24

17

I WILL HAVE FAITH

I will have faith so much so that even Jesus Christ will find no such faith in Israel.

Inspired by
Luke 7:9

I LIVE FEARLESSLY

I live fearlessly, trusting in Jesus Christ, knowing God's watchful eyes see that which I cannot see.

Inspired by
Luke 12:4

19

I PRIORITIZE THE KINGDOM

I prioritize the Kingdom of Heaven, preserving my life through letting go of the things of this world.

Inspired by
Luke 17:33

I PRAY THAT I STAY AWAKE

Although He is not here physically, I pray that I stay awake and enter not into temptation.

Inspired by
Luke 22:40

21

I PARTAKE OF THE WORD

I partake of The Word and in repentance receive forgiveness that I may be a testament of the gospel of Jesus Christ.

Inspired by
Luke 24:47

I COMPREHEND THE LIGHT

I comprehend The Light, allowing it to be my guide through the darkness which does not understand The Light.

Inspired by
John 1:5

23

I SPEAK FROM EXPERIENCE

I speak from my experience, that I know what Christ has done in my life and in the lives of others.

Inspired by
John 3:11

24

I RADIATE BURNING LIGHT

I radiate the burning light shining out of me, a reflection of who I call Lord, revealing The Way, The Life and The Truth.

Inspired by
John 5:35

25

I DO NOT JUDGE APPERANCES

I do not judge appearances, but judge the righteous judgement according to their works toward God and His Son.

Inspired by
John 7:24

26

I UNDERSTAND NOW

I understand now that healing is mine, no matter the time or place, in faith, Jesus Christ can open my eyes.

Inspired by
John 9:14

I EMBRACE THE LESSONS

As I humbly serve, I embrace the lessons of love and the path of humility and enlightenment.

Inspired by
John 13:12

28

I JOURNEY CARRYING PEACE

I journey carrying peace from
The Father, sharing the love
bestowed upon me.

Inspired by
John 20:21

29

I RECEIVE POWER

I receive power from the Holy Ghost, which has come to me through baptism that I may bare witness to all the Earth.

Inspired by
ACTS 1:8

I STAND, WALK, AND LEAP

As I rise from my trials, I stand, I walk, and I leap as I go, praising God.

Inspired by
ACTS 3:8

I OPEN MY EYES AND SEE

I open my eyes and see the divine presence that surrounds me, without fear, I declare Christ my King.

Inspired by
ACTS 7:56

32

I WILL JOURNEY

I will journey through my life as a good person, full of faith and being added unto by The Lord.

Inspired by
ACTS 11:24

I HEAD DIVINE WHISPERS

I heed divine whispers, aligning with God's will, journeying and feasting upon all that unfolds before me.

Inspired by
ACTS 18:21

I KEEP NOTHING BACK

I keep nothing back from what I have learned, openly sharing the words that have been shared with me by The Spirit of The Lord.

Inspired by
ACTS 20:20

I STAND FIRM

I stand firm and of good cheer, anchored in God's promise amid life's stormy seas.

Inspired by
Acts 27:25

I SERVE GOD

I serve God with my whole heart, offering prayers of gratitude for all who seek Him.

Inspired by
Romans 1:9

I RECEIVE

I receive the boundless grace and justification given to me through Jesus Christ, redeemed by His life.

Inspired by
Romans 3:24

38

I AM JUSTIFIED

I am justified and rejoice in God's grace, and through faith, find peace.

Inspired by
Romans 5:1

I MUST NOW SEEK BY FAITH

I must now seek by faith, for my works have caused me to stumble according to the law that was.

Inspired by
Romans 9:32

40

I ALLOW MY FAITH

I allow my faith to blossom through the teaching of God about His Son Jesus Christ.

Inspired by
Romans 10:17

41

I ACCEPT THROUGH HIM

In awe of His wisdom, I accept through Him, and to Him, all things are created and glorified.

Inspired by
Romans 11:36

I PURSUE PEACE

I pursue peace and build others up, fostering a community of love and understanding.

Inspired by
Romans 14:19

43

I SHARE HIS LOVE

United with others in Christ, I share His love so that we may be perfectly joined together in harmony.

Inspired by
1 Corinthians 1:10

44

I LAY A FOUNDATION OF LOVE

With divine guidance, I lay a foundation of love, creating a blessed foundation for others to build from.

Inspired by
1 Corinthians 3:10

I EMBODY LIBERATION

Choosing peace, I embody liberation, allowing for others to journey with a heart set free.

Inspired by
1 Corinthians 7:15

I SHARE

I share my gifts and talents willingly to honor God and if I do not honor God first, then I am a liar.

Inspired by
1 Corinthians 9:17

47

I ACHIEVE WHAT I LABOR

I recognize God's grace and strength within me and achieve what I labor for in love toward my God who is with me.

Inspired by
1 Corinthians 15:10

48

I GIVE THANKS UNTO GOD

Led by Christ, I give thanks unto God who makes The Lords work manifest in all places that I go.

Inspired by
2 Corinthians 2:14

I REFLECT THE HUMILITY

I reflect the humility of my existence, willingly sharing Christ's love abundantly.

Inspired by
2 Corinthians 4:5

I CULTIVATE A DEEP SENSE

I cultivate a deep sense of confidence in my spiritual journey with the divine, knowing I am not at home just yet.

Inspired by
2 Corinthians 5:8

I KNOW GODLY SORROW

I know Godly sorrow, that which has led me to repentance and salvation, not to be regretted, but celebrated in Christ.

Inspired by
2 Corinthians 7:10

I TAKE COURAGE

In harmony, I take courage upon the comfort of being one with God, embracing peace and love.

Inspired by
2 Corinthians 13:11

I SURRENDER

Aligned with grace, I surrender to my Savior, letting go of my past in honor of God's purpose for my life.

Inspired by
Galatians 2:18

I ACKNOWLEDGE THE LAW

I acknowledge the law was a teacher, guiding me to Christ for salvation through faith.

Inspired by
Galatians 3:24

I WILL REAP

I will reap what I sow, and today I sow goodness and mindfulness.

Inspired by
Galatians 6:7

I MAKE CHOICES

I make choices that allow me to be chosen and blameless before Jesus Christ.

Inspired by
Ephesians 1:4

I ACCEPT GRACE

I accept grace, the same grace that The Lord gives to all people, and I am willing to give others the same grace that I accept.

Inspired by
Ephesians 4:7

58

I AFFIRM THE LIGHT

I affirm The Light of The Truth, calling on Christ to cast out the dark work of those around me.

Inspired by
Ephesians 5:11

59

I CONDUCT MYSELF

I conduct myself in a manner worthy of the gospel, walking with The Lord, striving together in faith.

Inspired by
Philippians 1:27

I CONFESS EACH DAY

I confess each day, declaring that Jesus is The Lord and bow to His authority with gratitude and reverence.

Inspired by
Philippians 2:10

I TRANSFORM MY LIFE

I transform my life away from my past imperfections and toward the fashion of the body of God through His Son Jesus Christ.

Inspired by
Philippians 3:21

I HAVE ALL I NEED

I have all I need and am in abundance even to the state of fullness with God who accepts me.

Inspired by
Philippians 4:18

63

I WALK WORTHY

I walk worthy of The Lord, bearing fruit of every good work that I do, all while increasing my knowledge of God.

Inspired by
Colossians 1:10

I SET MY HEART

I set my heart on those things which are above, where Christ is, seated at the right hand of God.

Inspired by
Colossians 3:1

I KNOW HOW TO ANSWER

I know how to answer with grace, seasoning my life with The Word of God, now I know how to respond to life's trials.

Inspired by
Colossians 4:6

I NOW TURN FROM IDOLS

The gospels have shown the way, I now turn from idols and toward The Lord, who is the living and true God.

Inspired by
1 Thessalonians 1:9

67

I REJOICE IN HOPE

I rejoice in hope, joy and the crown of Jesus Christ, knowing He is coming.

Inspired by
1 Thessalonians 2:19

68

I AFFIRM LOVE

I affirm love as my guiding light, embracing the bond that unites all of us.

Inspired by
1 Thessalonians 4:9

69

I AM WORTHY

I am worthy of this calling, fulfilled with the good pleasure of His goodness, and now I act in faithfulness.

Inspired by
2 Thessalonians 1:11

I WANT

I want what God has given me,
the love and everlasting comfort
of good home through grace.

Inspired by
2 Thessalonians 2:16

I HAVE CONFIDENCE

I have confidence that the Lord does touch the things which I do, even as I do the things I am commanded to do.

Inspired by
2 Thessalonians 3:4

I ACKOWLEDGE THERE IS ONE

I acknowledge there is one God
and one Mediator between
God and humanity, He is
Christ Jesus, My Lord.

Inspired by
1 Timothy 2:5

I AM NOT HASTY

I am not hasty in the desires of others, and do not share in their sins, keeping myself pure.

Inspired by
1 Timothy 5:22

I TAKE HOLD

Fighting the good fight of faith, I take hold of eternal life and accept this truth before many witnesses.

Inspired by
1 Timothy 6:12

I THANK GOD

I thank God for my ancestors who have paved a path to this day, with my sincere heart, I offer gratitude for my heritage.

Inspired by
2 Timothy 1:3

I CHOOSE TO FOLLOW

Alongside those who seek the Lord with pure hearts, I choose to follow righteousness, faith, charity, and peace.

Inspired by
2 Timothy 2:22

I SEEK AFTER A CROWN

I seek after a crown of righteousness which The Lord has prepare for me, but not only me, for all who love Him.

Inspired by
2 Timothy 4:8

I HAVE HOPE

I have hope of eternal life, the promise made by God before the foundation of the Earth, the God that cannot lie.

Inspired by
Titus 1:2

I HAVE BEEN TAUGHT

I have been taught to deny
ungodliness and worldly lusts,
that I will live soberly, righteously
and Godly in this world.

Inspired by
Titus 2:12

I SHOULD BE AN HEIR

Having been justified by His grace, I should be an heir of The Kingdom, having hope for eternal life.

Inspired by
Titus 3:7

81

I COMMUNICATE ACTIVELY

I communicate actively by acknowledging all the good that is in me, which is in Jesus Christ.

Inspired by
Philemon 1:6

82

I SHALL HAVE JOY

I shall have joy in The Lord, who will refresh my bowels.

Inspired by
Philemon 1:20

I WILL AGAIN TRUST HIM

I will again trust Him, behold I am a child of God, as are those who are in my life.

Inspired by
Hebrews 2:13

I DECLARE HIM MY SAVIOR

I declare Him my Savior and King, from the foundation of the Earth, He gives me rest.

Inspired by
Hebrews 4:3

I HAVE THE SUBSTANCE

Now in faith, I have the substance of all things hoped for, with no need for the evidence of things seen.

Inspired by
Hebrews 11:1

I AM EQUIPPTED

I am equipped with everything good for aligning with the will of God, and I do that which is good in His eyes.

Inspired by
Hebrews 13:21

I ASK FROM GOD

I ask from God, to deliver all things which I lack wisdom of, knowing it is God who gives generously without finding fault in me.

Inspired by
James 1:5

I FIND PURITY AND PEACE

In the wisdom from above, I find purity and peace, being gentle, I show mercy without hypocrisy.

Inspired by
James 3:17

89

I SIN NO MORE

I sin no more, knowing what is right, I shall do that which I know to do.

Inspired by
James 4:17

I AM KEPT SAFE

I am kept safe by the power of God, through faith, I am ready to be revealed.

Inspired by
1 Peter 1:5

I WISH TO BE OF ONE MIND

I wish to be of one mind with His chosen people, having compassion and love with a tender heart toward all.

Inspired by
1 Peter 3:8

I GREET EACH DAY

I greet each day with a kiss of love, accepting the peace that comes with Jesus Christ.

Inspired by
1 Peter 5:14

I MAKE EVERY EFFORT

I make every effort to confirm my callings are made elect, and that in all things I do, I shall never stumble.

Inspired by
2 Peter 1:10

I HOPE TO BE DELIEVERED

I hope to be delivered out of temptations, to be of God, so that I remain just at the day of judgment.

Inspired by
2 Peter 2:9

95

I HONOR GOD

I honor God who keeps His promise, and look forward to a new heaven and new earth, where I will dwell in righteousness.

Inspired by
Peter 3:13

I HAVE SEEN AND HEARD

I have seen and heard the Truth, now declaring it to others in fellowship with the Father and His Son Jesus Christ.

Inspired by
1 John 1:3

I WILL NOT BE DECEIVED

I will not deceived, knowing that only those who do righteousness are righteous, even as Christ is righteous.

Inspired by
1 John 3:7

I LOVE OTHERS

I love others knowing love is of God, and those that love others are born of God and know God.

Inspired by
1 John 4:7

99

I ACCEPT

From the Father and The Son, I accept grace, mercy, peace, truth, and love.

Inspired by
2 John 1:3

100

I LOOK FOR MYSELF

I look at myself, that I will not lose the things which I have accomplished, that I may receive my full reward.

Inspired by
2 John 1:8

I PRAY

I pray in all respects that I may prosper and be in good health, just as my soul prospers.

Inspired by
3 John 1:2

I FOLLOW NOT EVIL

I follow not evil, rather I embrace that which is good, things which only come from The Father.

Inspired by
3 John 1:11

I PAY NO ATTENTION

I pay no attention to the scoffers or the mockers of God, for their own god is their lusts and desires.

Inspired by
Jude 1:18

I LOOK FOR MERCY

Keeping myself in the love of God, I look for mercy of the Lord Jesus Christ unto eternal life.

Inspired by
Jude 1:21

I OVERCOME ALL THINGS

I overcome all things and will sit on the throne of God, along with Jeus Christ who has also overcame all things.

Inspired by
Revelation 3:21

I MAY APPEAR OVERCOME

I may appear overcome by sickness, but I will rise with the Spirit of Life from God once more.

Inspired by
Revelation 11:11

I SIGN THE SONG

I sing the song of Moses, The song of The Servant, the song of The Lamb. honoring the great and marvelous works of The Almighty.

Inspired by
Revelation 15:3

I FALL TO WORSHIP

I fall to worship Him and hear the words, "I am thy fellow servant, worship God and testify of Jesus as the Spirit of prophecy"

Inspired BY
Revelation 19:10

109

I AM A NEW HEART

I am a new heart, a new Heaven, a new Earth, and my former self has passed away.

Inspired by
Revelation 21:1

110

I LET THEM BE

I let them be, those who are unjust, be unjust, those who are filthy, be filthy, those who are righteous, be righteous, those who are holy, be holy.

Inspired by
Revelation 22:11

111

I TAKE UPON THE GRACE

Amen, I take upon the grace of the Lord Jesus Christ, to allow it to be with those who choose it.

Inspired by
Revelation 22:21

My aim in writing these affirmations was to create a space where readers could find inspiration, reflection, and a sense of spiritual connection. Your decision to explore these affirmations from The New Testament means the world to me, and I hope they bring moments of peace, encouragement, and personal growth to your life as you journey on.

MATTHEW LUKE WEBSTER

Made in the USA
Columbia, SC
26 January 2024

30054680R00065